I0536581

So Ya Wanna Sleep With Broke Sperm!

ISBN: 978-1-971419-18-3

Darling dear, gather round,
I was sent to fix dating since WOMEN burned it down.

Your love life's a mess, and we all know why —
Some women date like ho's... or worse — a gay guy.

I'll give you two rules — it's not rocket science,
To stop getting used and start getting compliance.

Follow them, darling — I promise, you'll win.
But first... let's see how this mess all began.

In caveman days, men would hunt and provide,
Proudly cared for the woman by his side.

Brave and strong — her armor, her shield,
Food on the table from the hunt in the field.

Now men hunt for hookups, expect dinner on you —
Free sex, free meals... and they ghost when they're through.

Moving forward, women had grace —
Men had to court to get to first base.

Women were ladies — they'd wait, not sway.
"No marriage? No sex," is what they'd say.

Then feminism made hookups the trend...
Now good women can't find decent men.

Now, Gloria cried, "Be free! You don't need no guy!"
While she cashed CIA checks — now ask yourself why.

Wake up, darlings — you were played in that trick,
By women on payrolls from someone with a dick.

The files are released — the receipts don't deceive,
Yet women still clap... because they were brainwashed to believe.

Back in the day we had tea and time—life felt right and fair.
Now 33% of women report deep loneliness they can't repair.

Anxiety's 23%, depression's up for sure.
Panic disorder hits 3.8%—twice what men endure.

Alcohol misuse surged 84%—that's more than just stress.
Once we acted like ladies—now it's
Zoloft, boxed wine, and mess.

"I'm a modern woman! We're equal!
I can lay and pay!"
No you're not, dear — that's a dumb thing to say.

Did he spend two hours getting hair/nails and dressed?
While bleeding, cramping, and hormonally stressed?

You're picturing vows, a ring, a sweet life —
He's picturing you naked... not as his wife.

Some modern women fear sugar and tap water, you see,
But risks STDs with whoever feels free.

Buys non-toxic shampoo, organic kale —
The irony? Tracks toxins with holy detail.

She bans seed oils, calls chemicals sin,
But not a man's junk or what he shoots in!

"My body, my choice," says the girl with no esteem,
Who sleeps with ten men, says it don't mean a thing.

Then posts on her story, "Living my truth!"
While choking down tears in a therapy booth.

Xanax and wine and a cheap cotton dress —
Darling, that's not freedom. That's a mental mess.

Young women brag about body count like it's a prize,
But they weren't designed to be used by four guys.

They drink, they vape, pop pills to feel sane,
While swiping for love that just ends in pain.

Thery're "successful" — but crying alone in their bed.
Darlings, if you won't fix dating? Then suffer instead.

Prostitutes lost their jobs — we all know why.
Desperate, lonely girls swipe yes to any guy.

Back then, at least hookers got paid —
Cash on the dresser, a fair trade was made.

It claimed to empower — now look what it's done...
Even sex for survival's been ruined for fun.

How did we get here? What a tragic twist.
We give men everything — is emotional damage worth the risk?

She dreams of connection, gives all she's got —
He shows up with crumbs, and thinks that's a lot.

She's tired, disheartened, still comes when he calls —
Yet THE BAD MEN think they are the victim in it all.

If he were dating Margot Robbie, he'd show up on time,
Reservations booked, jacket, flowers—prime.

He'd grab the check—no math, no split,
No "gold-digger" smear—no acting like a dimwit.

Talk plans, talk future, treat you like the prize—
If he won't do that for you, cut the damn ties.

This isn't one of the two rules ahead,
'Cause most of you won't wait — you'll hop in his bed.

IMAGINE... if we all held out for a diamond ring,
We'd change the whole miserable dating thing.

If he leaves? That sucks! But that diamond pays,
For Botox, Bahamas, and 10 bawling days.

What's the one thing that can fix this whole mess?
The old-fashioned rule: don't get undressed!

"No sex" used to work — so now what's the play?
Since "wait 'til marriage" won't fly today...

I got you, dear — just follow my lead:
It weeds out BAD MEN and gets rings with speed.

RULE ONE

Men hate condoms — yeah, women do too,
But they stay on 'til he says "I do."

He'll moan and complain, he'll pout and protest,
But keeping it wrapped is for YOUR best.

He'll say you're "no fun" or "killing the mood,"
But discipline's hotter than being used.

No ring? No risk. That's how it's done.
The condom stays on — until you're the one.

Now darlings, beware — you've got to stay smart,
He'll say, "It won't stay up with a cover on my part."

Or, "Condoms make me itch! I'm allergic, I swear!"
"My therapist says I need skin-to-skin care!"

OR IT'S, "We've dated a year — I want just you…"
Lovely. The condom comes off when you say "I do."

You let broke sperm cum inside of you?
You work hard — and that's what you chose to do!!!!!!

There's IUDs, the patch, Plan B, a shot,
Condoms, the pill — girl, you had a lot.

He got an orgasm and snuck out like a thief —
You could be left to give birth... or kill whatever your belief.

You can't risk your health for a man who won't commit —
Condoms protect from nefarious shit.

Feminism said, "Be free, explore and play!"
But is catching chlamydia the empowered way?

Equal? Please. That BS needs to die.
He won't get yeast, BV, or PID — oh my.

RULE TWO

No commitment until there's a ring —
That's how we bring back the marriage thing.

Date Steve, date Larry, even that guy Harry —
You're not exclusive 'til he wants to marry.

If he doesn't want you with anyone else in your bed,
Then he should put a ring on your finger instead.

Men won't tell you you're not the one —
They'll sleep with you 'til the fun is done.

He'll take your years, your body, your care —
But when he meets "her," you'll vanish —
poof — air.

I know when you like him, you don't want to stray,
But date other men — it must be that way.

You can't get attached 'til you know he's all in —
Not just playing the field with a confident grin.

If he's in love, he won't let it slide —
He'll lock it down fast, with no games to hide.

But if he's just using you, or sleeping around...
He won't care who you f*ck — let that truth resound.

Date 'til engaged — don't fall for "Let's see..."
Men get hotter with time — women age out, sadly.

He'll waste your best years just passing through —
Then marry a 25-year-old when he's 42.

No ring, no claim — he's full of 💩.
If he doesn't want you dating other men — he'll make it legit.

If you're too insecure to stand your ground,
Then don't date — you'll just be passed around.

You teach a man how to treat you, babe —
So if HE'S setting the rules, you're being played!

If your self-respect made him flee the room,
Lucky you — he's not your groom.

Got pregnant from a stranger, now you're off to court.
You're successful, now you pay him child support.

Or, didn't even climax from your little fling,
And left with an itchy, burning thing.

Thought he liked you — turns out not true,
Just used for sex, through and through.

Men and women aren't equal, it's plain to see —
Lessen your risk, and listen to me.

Men bond with vasopressin — that's how it's done,
NOT from quick sex, or a random night's fun.

If he's not connected before he gets laid,
It's dopamine only — NO bond being made.

Competing with porn, with PlayStation, with hos —
That's dopamine, darling — and everyone but you knows.

You're weeping, repeating, "He'll change — give it time,"
While his brain says, "Next!" — and he ghosts on a dime.

Sex is different — that much is clear.
Guys do it for fun, women bond, my dear.

Girls who claim they don't care? That's a mental disguise —
It's daddy issues, trauma, or a cocktail of lies.

Oxytocin is real — it'll glue you to the wrong guy.
We weren't built for hookups — your hormones don't comply.

"I know it's hard, but darling, it's true —
Low standards won't get a ring for you."

A gentleman won't whine when you set the tone,
He'll say, "She's the one," and make you his own.

Be whiny, pleasy, a pick-me thing —
It's pathetic, darling — men marry the queen.

When men see you've got class and strong rules,
You stand out from the promiscuous fools.

You're the one they want — rare and refined,
Not another girl they did from behind.

No pregnancy scares, no STIs…
Just a unicorn glow that draws good guys.

WARNING!

Women should take dating more seriously.
The wrong man will destroy you — fast and mercilessly.

"Don't live off a man!" — that's what they say,
So you busted your ass and got that MBA.

Now here comes divorce — you worked to the bone,
He met some new woman, you have to buy them a home.

The irony's thick — society cheers, "Yay!"
While you pay a man, in menopause, sweating each day.

RECAP

RULE ONE: No condom off the D.
If you're not engaged, there's no entry.

RULE TWO: No exclusivity till there's a ring.
You keep dating — times have changed, darling.

You've got goals, class, and real pedigree —
So don't let noncommittal sperm touch luxury.

The KELLY MEGYN SHOW

FNN News

Breaking: Ghost's dating rules are going viral—men are nervous!

Grab your big-girl panties — you know what's in store,
Men will flip out when they can't give you crumbs no more.

They'll sneer "you're too much!" or "gold digger," they say —
That's not a husband, dear — run the f*ck away.

A real man will nod: "I'll respect you, stay true.
I won't ghost, won't mistreat, won't make you feel blue."

"I've got a sister — I want men to treat her well.
Men who use women? Disgusting. They can go to hell."

So don't be dumb — don't waste your prime.
Words mean nothing if actions don't align.

If you give your all while he's still vetting,
You'll be heartbroken — not getting a wedding.

This will work, just wait and see...
Break these rules? Don't come crying to me.

And here's the last thing I'll say:
Why would anyone change if it's all going their way?

Thank you from the bottom of my heart for reading my book.
I love and admire all women, and my greatest wish is for each of you to
find joy, confidence, and lasting love with a truly good man who values
and cherishes you.
If you enjoyed this book, it would mean the world to me if you left a
review.
And while you're there, I'd love for you to share one piece of dating
advice that has worked for you — something that could inspire and
help other women on their own journey.
Your story, your wisdom, and your voice matter.
Let's help each other write happier love stories.
With love,

-G